The ~~Little~~ "BIG" Book of Daytime Illusions

A coloring book illustrated by
Kevin James

the fuchsian gallery company
from Kevin James

Book Design: Kevin James
Manufactured in the USA.

A word from Kevin James:

Hi there! The Little Book, I mean The BIG Book of Daytime Illusions is really something to appreciate. The "Daytime Illusions" series from me represents more than just pictures. These are all raw, in the moment illustrations that have been composed into each and every book. What you're getting is not only an experience to enhance your imagination with images from my own; you're getting hand-drawn to book illustrations to color and share with your family. Isn't that cool? Now, you have the floor.

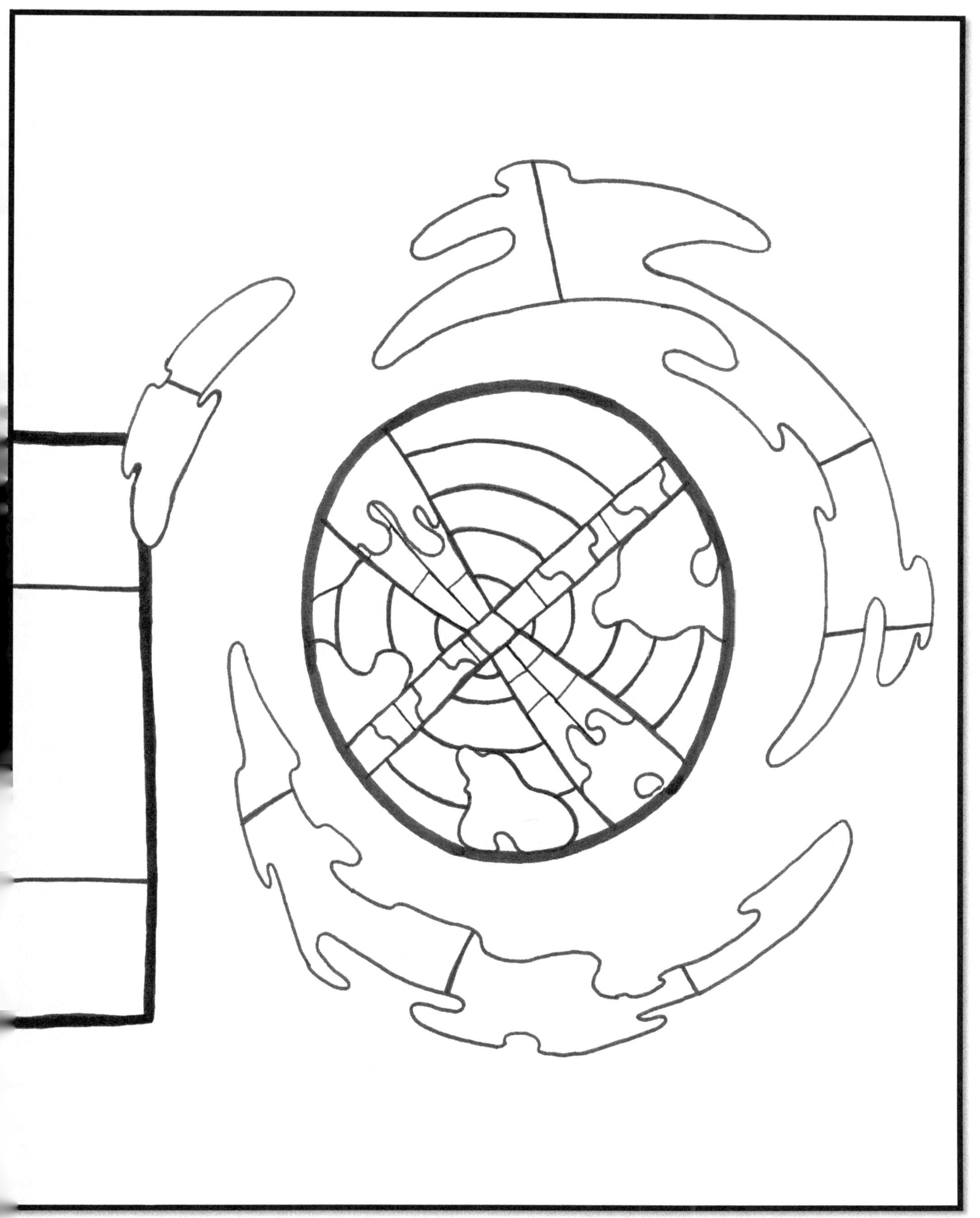

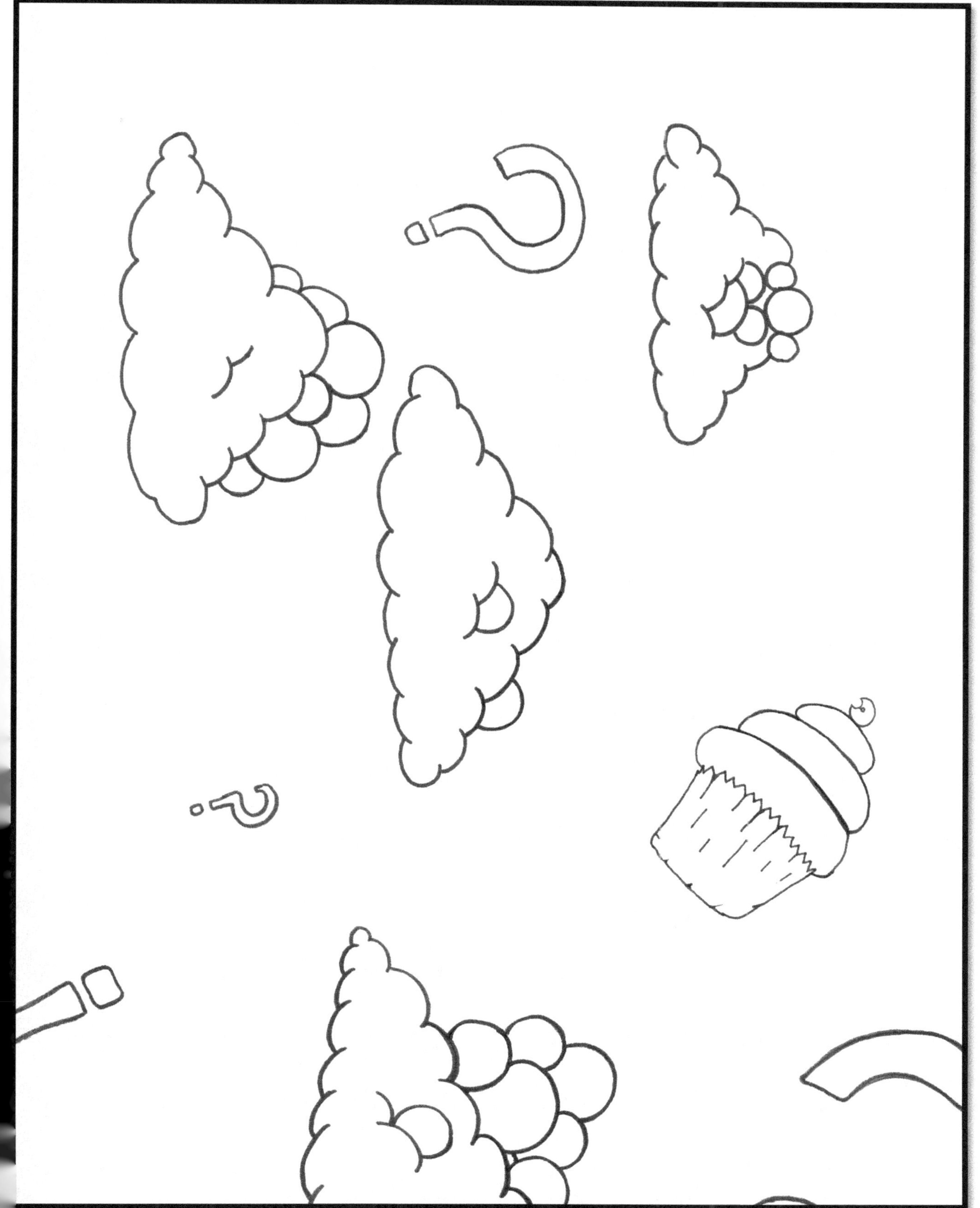

Whew!

You did it! Did you see that rollercoaster you had to tackle? Imagine illustrating it! Did you have a blast sailing the high seas, exploring castles, and illustrating your own face? This is the end of The BIG Book of Daytime Illusions, will there be another? Perhaps. I'm glad that you had fun. I had fun making the book for you. See you again!

- Kevin James

This is our 20th book! See more:

www.fuchsiangalleryco.com

the fuchsian gallery company
from Kevin James

The Little Book of Daytime Illusions 1
The Little Book of Daytime Illusions: Two and Through
Both available everywhere books are sold.
The Fuchsian Gallery Company 2017
"The fusion between colors and ideas."

www.ingramcontent.com/pod-product-compliance
Lightning Source LLC
Chambersburg PA
CBHW080733260726
48660CB00010B/3816